21 Crucial Things They Don't Teach Young People About Sex

By Tony Peters

Published by
T P PUBLICATIONS
4 Pegamoid Road.
Edmonton. London.
N18 2NG

Copyright © 2021 by Tony Peters

ISBN 978-1-874332-65-7

I dedicate this book to my Lover
& Best Friend, Shola Peters;
And to my two inimitable children,
Anthony and Melody – who give me plenty
of reasons to want to invest in the
next generation...

TABLE OF CONTENT

Preface

This is my humble attempt to give the young people of this generation an unpadded, no-nonsense book on the foolishness of a sexually perverted philosophy of life.

I want you to see clearly that not everything in the culture you live in is good, appropriate, or even healthy for you. I have no doubt that there are some positive elements in our cultural evolution, but the harmful stuff within it heavily outweighs the good stuff – a hundred to one.

People often ridicule the idea of moral standards in a heavily sexualised culture, but those moral standards have served previous generations well. I contend that they will not only serve you better today, but would place the good life you've always wanted on a platter before you.

More importantly, is the issue of what our Creator has to say about our sexual choices! After all, He made us with these desires and needs. Surely, then, He must know what works best; and if He does, we owe it to ourselves to discover and learn it.

So, in the rest of this book, we will endeavour to unveil the wisdom behind God's ageless blueprint, and expose the poison our culture is selling to young people when it comes to their sexual choices. Enjoy the ride!

There is a sense in which sexual sins are different from all others. In sexual sin we violate the sacredness of our own bodies.

(1 Corinthians 6:18. MSG.)

Introduction

A few decades ago, a number of Cigarette and Tobacco manufacturers allegedly destroyed the results of their own research that proved beyond doubt, that smoking was a health hazard.

At the time, there were rumours and accusations that these unscrupulous companies got rid of the evidence they had collected because it would have damaged their industry, if it were released to the general public.

Since then, unfortunately, tens of millions of people all over the world have suffered major health challenges and even painful deaths because they were denied the facts before they got hooked on smoking. Fortunately, we now know the facts.

- We now know that:
- Smoking causes cancer.
- It damages our lungs.
- It weakens our immunity.
- It hurts our unborn children.
- It destroys our white blood cells.
- It stains our teeth & makes our breath stink.
- It affects the efficiency of our internal organs, and
- It reduces our life expectancy – to mention a few known consequences of this additive habit.

We now know that this damning information was covered up or destroyed. And, the question is why? How could these tobacco manufacturers deceive millions of fun loving people, Governments, and even Nations?

A number of reasons come to mind, that all centre on money and the love of money. These tobacco manufacturers controlled ridiculous amounts of money; and with their money, they were able to make 'things' disappear.

Sadly, these anomalies are still with us today. Many of our political leaders, health workers and media moguls know what I am about to share with you in this book, but most would prefer to keep it from you if they could.

They know that as long as the general population stays ignorant, money will keep flowing into their coffers. Our young people will keep destroying their bodies, their minds and their future. Pharmaceutical giants will keep getting fat. And, negligent governments will keep getting elected into office.

Our policy makers, medical thinkers, and political leaders know a lot that they are not telling us. They don't want the heat. For them, it is important to stick with the party line and not rock the boat. It is also more important to stay politically correct than to correctly educate the masses of young people who are falling prey to the diabolic lies of our enemy.

I care what happens to you because I am a 'shepherd' and a 'pastor' at heart. I love God and I love people. My heart reaches across the continents to everyone who, in God's providence, will pick up this book.

My prayer is that it would help you make the right decisions about your sexual choices and your future - because (whether you like it or not) your sexual choices will affect your future one way or the other.

If this book in some small way helps you make godly decisions that are right for you, my job here is done. But your job has just begun. And that job is to help as many young people as you can in your generation to break free from the lies that are being presented to them by their lecturers, the mass Media and by Hollywood.

21 Important things Hollywood, the Media, Secular Health Professionals and those who control the flow of information will not tell you about Sex

#1

An Amazing Sex Life

**God wants you to have an amazing sex life –
as long as it is with the right person
at the right time.**

Who is the right person? The right person is the one who is committed to you in sickness and in health, whether you are rich or poor, till death do you part.

The right person is the man who has met your parents; asked for your hand in marriage; and put a ring on your finger in front of a minister and in the presence of your family and friends.

The right person is the lady who loves and respects you enough to come alongside you and help you reach your destiny – even if that means putting some parts of her ambitions on hold for a while.

God created sex to be enjoyed in the context of a loving, committed, responsible, and stable marriage relationship. So the right time is when you get married. In that context, sex is beautiful and uplifting. Anything outside of this ideal is fraught with guilt and trouble.

Hollywood wants you to believe that it's okay to jump into bed with anyone who makes you feel good. That's why millions of dollars are spent every year making cheesy movies to indoctrinate and programme the minds of impressionable young people.

The problem with this philosophy of life is that it ignores the fact that sex ties you to the other person - spiritually, emotionally, and physically. Sex ties your souls together, and soul-ties are hard (if not impossible) to break.

Soul-ties are difficult to break because a piece of you (that is, the essence of who you are) is always left with or in anyone you sleep with, and a piece of them is always left in or with you.

People may argue as to whether this happens physically, emotionally, or spiritually, but there is no denying that it happens when two people share the most intimate part of themselves.

On the other hand, sex in the context of a loving marriage is like the icing on the cake. It's like a piece of heaven on earth. There is no guilt, no fears of insecurity or getting pregnant, no hiding from your parents or peers, and no worries that your partner would take advantage of you and dump you if you don't perform to their standard.

The media will not tell you that God wants you to enjoy amazing sex with the right person in the context of a committed marriage relationship, because that would reduce the money they generate from a perverse culture of sexual exploitation.

If you want to please God and have the future you've always dreamed of, your axiom should be "Sex after marriage is the icing on the cake, sex before marriage is usually a bad mistake."

2

Doing the Unthinkable

Sex outside of marriage leads to more than 90% of all abortions and unwanted pregnancies - in the world.

Over 6 million abortions are estimated to occur around the world every year. That averages at over 16,400 abortion procedures a day. Some preformed by quacks and others performed by well-regulated clinics.

But, irrespective of who is doing the procedures, we are not only wasting billions of pounds paying for these (often barbaric) procedures, but we are destroying and throwing away vast amounts of human potential.

Who knows how many of these babies could have grown to be a Mother Theresa, or a Nelsen Mandela, or a Billy Graham, or a Mary Slessor, or an Albert Einstein?

Unfortunately, the massacre is not likely to change any time soon, because there are multinational companies with billions of pounds that have a vested interest in things staying the way they are.

Why are we having so many unwanted children in the first place? Well, the answer is simple. We are indulging in too much sex outside of marriage. We have constructed a culture that says, "It's okay to sleep with whoever you fancy." Sadly, the consequence is too many unnecessary abortions.

Just think about it:

16,400 healthy children aborted every day because we want to have fun and not handle the consequences of our actions.

16,400 innocent, viable infants slaughtered daily because we have bought into a decadent culture of sexual exploitation.

16,400 healthy babies aborted daily because we think we are wiser than the God who created us and gave us our sex organs.

6,000,000 vulnerable babies deliberately torn from their mother's womb every year because they are too tiny to fight for themselves, and the people who should be fighting for them are more interested in partying or staying slim.

With the help of Hollywood and the mass Media, we have rejected the traditional values of marriage and chastity – that worked so well for our ancestors – and have embraced a degenerate culture that encourages immorality and utter disregard for life.

Surprisingly, when a madman walks into a school and shoots and kills 20 children, we all gnash our teeth against him in derision, while we do the same thing to 6,000,000 unborn children (nearly every year) and pat ourselves on the back for getting away with it.

Sex outside of marriage is directly responsible for most of these innocent deaths. I shudder to think of how God must feel about these deliberate crimes against so much viable human life. I shudder to think of what we would say when the 'souls' of these unwanted babies ask us why we deprived them of life. May God have mercy on us!

The 'powers that be' in our society are not keen to warn you of the dangers of indiscriminate sex outside of marriage, because a lot of expensive contracts will dry up and a lot of abortion clinics will shut down.

I, on the other hand, have no qualms telling you the truth as I see it, because I don't want you to be ignorant. In the end, what you choose to do about it is your decision. Choose wisely!

#3

Fear of Getting Pregnant

Those who educate young people will not tell you that:

Fear of getting pregnant or getting caught reduces the pleasure and satisfaction that sex is designed to give you.

In a teenage survey carried out some years ago, 8 out of 10 teenage girls admitted to not really enjoying their sexual experiences. When they were asked why they were doing something that they didn't enjoy, some said they only did it as a favour or because their boy friend put pressure on them to have sex.

How sad! It is a well-know fact that people don't enjoy doing anything if they are feeling guilty, worried, or scared. That is why the majority of teenage or underage sex is unfulfilling – especially among the girls.

So if you are a girl reading this book, my advice to you is *don't do sexual favours—they make you cheap.* You are unlikely to enjoy it anyway, because of worry, guilt, shame, or fear. Also, you may end up under more pressure to do something you would never have wanted to do – like terminating your own baby's life or giving your baby up for adoption.

Keep yourself for the young man who wants all of you, not just a piece of you. If you are chaste, the right guy will show up in time. But if you allow yourself to be used, your self-esteem will suffer and, chances are, you will continue to attract guys who only want to use you for the rest of your life.

To the guys, I say: Don't let your temporary sexual urges make you responsible for the life of a child you are not ready for, or the death of a child you do not want. Those who have not yielded to this advice in the past carry deep-rooted regrets that never really go away.

Don't pressure any girl into having sex with you if you are not married to her, because the consequences for disobeying God's instructions are severe. Remember that one day you will stand before God; and you won't be able to say you didn't know or were not warned.

I advise you to have friends of the opposite sex and learn to enjoy their company. I will even encourage you to go out together with the opposite sex in groups of different sizes. That is all you need from the opposite sex until you are ready for a serious relationship that would hopefully end in a marriage proposal.

For more help in this area, check out my book titled: **Say Goodbye to Dating** - Find Your Soul Mate God's Way.

Avoid being exclusive with anyone if you are not ready to commit. And, avoid being on your own in compromising places with the opposite sex. Why? Because one foolish slip is all it takes to ruin a good thing. One silly decision is all it takes to sabotage your future.

The media and professionals will not tell that your state of mind out of wedlock is more likely to hinder sexual pleasure, because they really want you to believe that the opposite is true. They want you to believe (as is shown in almost every block buster film) that every sexual encounter will lead to bouts of ecstasy.

It's a lie! Don't fall for it!! Doing the wrong thing never produces the right results. And that's true for every facet of life!

<h1 style="text-align:center">#4</h1>

<h1 style="text-align:center">Below the Poverty Line</h1>

Those who educate young people will not tell you that:

Premarital sex increases your risk of getting pregnant, dropping out of school, becoming a single parent, and living below the poverty line for the best part of your life.

That is precisely what is happening to the majority of young girls who are getting pregnant out of wedlock in our society. They drop out of fulltime education and either look for a low paying job that's flexible enough to accommodate the children or stay on welfare for extended periods of time.

More often than not, their education suffers, their self-esteem takes a battering, and their quality of life drops below the poverty line. Sadly, many are estranged from their parents or alienated from the child's other parent, or both.

Either way, too many young people are short-changed in life. Today, in the UK, there are over 2,000,000 single parent families. And, although their circumstances and stories are very different, the majority of them are just managing to stay afloat financially.

My point is simply this: Having a child out of wedlock is not glamorous. It is hard. It affects you in more ways than you

18

can imagine. And, child-rearing was designed to work better with two loving and committed parents.

Premarital sex, with its consequences, often drags its victims into a vicious cycle of poverty, pain, struggle and disappointment. The media will not tell you that premarital sex has this kind of effect on thousands of people every year, because they don't really care what happens to you, so long as they get the scoop on your 'riches-to-rags' story.

God cares that you enjoy everything you were born to enjoy while you are here. He wants you to have the spouse of your dreams, the home you've always wanted, and the children that would carry your legacy into the future. If that is what you want for yourself, nothing and nobody but you, can stop it from materialising in time.

Don't follow the masses if you want a better life for yourself and your children. Follow the One who promises to give you life more abundantly. His name is Jesus the Christ; and His agenda is to give you a beautiful life here and hereafter.

That's what He has done for me, and hundreds of people I know personally. And, that's what He will do for you if you heed His instructions.

Jesus said:

> *"Yes, I am the gate. Those who come in through me will be saved. They will come and go freely and will find good pastures. The thief's purpose is to steal and kill and destroy. My purpose is to give them a rich and satisfying life. "I am the good shepherd. The good shepherd sacrifices his life for the sheep.*

> (John 10:9-11.) NLT.

Trust in the Lord with all your heart; do not depend on your own understanding. Seek his will in all you do, and he will show you which path to take. Don't be impressed with your own wisdom.
Instead, fear the Lord and turn away from evil. Then you will have healing for your body and strength for your bones.

(Proverbs 3:5-8.) NLT.

<h1 align="center">#5</h1>

Can't Have Children

Some young ladies (and men) can't have children of their own because of the careless sexual choices they made when they were younger.

One of the very sad consequences of premarital sex is the devastation that happens when things really go wrong. That is, when, for instance, an abortion goes wrong. A pregnancy goes wrong. An infection due to poor hygiene ravages parts of the body. Or, worse still, when someone is infected with the HIV - Aids virus.

Sometimes a sexually transmitted disease (STD) can damage the lady's womb or the man's ability to produce sufficient sperm. These problems and more can damage parts of the reproductive system and leave some couples disappointed for life when they really want children.

It seems foolish to jeopardise your future happiness for 5 minutes of fun. I don't pray that this should happen to you, but I have a responsibility to let you know that it happens— and that when it does, it may lead to untold misery.

Remember that, when you sleep with someone, you are inadvertently sleeping with all the people they have slept with. If any of those people had a disease, it could easily be passed on to you.

The media may not want to tell you this, as there is no sure way of knowing how many couples can't have children naturally due to the problems mentioned above. But if there is a mere one-in-ten thousand chance that this could happen to you, I owe it to you to tell you the truth.

Don't mess up your reproductive organs or your future happiness for a few minutes of muted fun. That would be tragic and sad!

#6

Don't Open Pandora's Box

Those who educate young people will not tell you that:

Once your sex-drive has been aroused, it's very difficult to control or stop it.

I have been told that girls find it easier to resist sex if they don't like it or want it. It is not so for boys. Once a guy starts to engage in sexual activity, it is much harder for him to control the desire. He almost always wants more sex and goes to extraordinary lengths to get it.

Sex for guys is like a drug. We get addicted to it. We want more of it; and we often evaluate our manhood by how much of it we get.

Some guys even get withdrawal symptoms if they've not had sex for a few days. That is why arousing a boy's sexual interest too soon can be precarious.

A guy can go for 25 years without badly needing sex, but once that urge is unleashed, it's very difficult to control it without discipline and God's help.

A wise man once said, "Sex is like the ocean—the more you get into it, the further away from the shore you get and the more difficult it becomes to swim back to shore on your own."

Why? Because sex can be addictive! It can create an unhealthy appetite for more sex – without the mutual commitment that tempers and moderates it.

Experts estimate that by the time a boy – who started having sex at 16 – reaches the age of 25, he would have had 6 or more sexual partners, on average. A good percentage of young boys have a lot more!

Wanting more sex is not the worst thing that can happen when sexual urges are unfettered; it's the hurts that accompany it that concern me. It's the broken hearts!

It's the sexually transmitted diseases! It's the loss of young people's virginity to the wrong person! It's the psychological pain and the sense of abuse young people feel! That's the big concern here.

It is true that, as people get older, they are often better able to control or manage their sexual urges. Unfortunately, controlling the sexual urge is not that easy when you are young. So don't get it started until you have sealed your relationship with a lifetime commitment.

If you've already started having regular sex, but you are not married to your partner, speak to someone who can help you with some spiritual or practical advice.

Also, ask God to help you control the urge and focus your energises elsewhere. You will never regret doing the right thing, and you will save yourself from a lot of trouble.

The media and the pharmaceutical companies want you to think that having sex is just harmless fun, but it isn't. Someone almost always gets hurt. Someone's life-plan almost always gets derailed. And, you always displease God in the process. That cannot be good for any thoughtful person. That is not the path you want to take either.

God's will for your life is clear:

Do not let sin control the way you live; do not give in to its lustful desires. Do not let any part of your body become a tool of wickedness, to be used for sinning. Instead, give yourselves completely to God since you have been given new life. And use your whole body as a tool to do what is right for the glory of God.

(Romans 6:12-13.) NLT

#7

The Safe Sex Myth

There's no such thing as Safe Sex

The phrase 'safe sex' is used a lot to give young people the impression that they can try out sex with any number of partners in a totally safe and risk-free way. Unfortunately, many young people have bought into this lie.

The truth, however, is that every time you have sex, you are at risk of getting pregnant (or impregnating your partner). You are at risk of contracting a Sexually Transmitted Disease (STD), and becoming emotionally or psychologically scarred. That is a fact!

Even when you use the best available condoms, there are still risks. Condom manufacturers now acknowledge that condom safety can be as low as 95%. That means there is up to a 1 in 20 chance that your condom will burst, leak, not be worn properly, or come off during sex.

Some years ago, I read a report on the safety of condoms, and I was shocked at what I read. Here are a couple of statements from the experts:

"One million people a day will be exposed to sexually transmitted diseases and unwanted pregnancies unless improvements are made in condom safety, experts have warned."

Julian Edwards, the then-Director General of Consumers International said, "...If a breakage rate of 5% becomes the norm, more than a million extra exposures to Aids and unwanted pregnancies would occur every single day."

Even if they are able to increase the safety rate of condoms, it can't protect you from the emotional or psychological battles that often follow early sexual encounters among young people.

For instance, condoms can't protect you from the guilt, the shame, the losing of your virginity to a guy who no longer wants you, the struggle to concentrate on your studies, the horrible things people say about each other when they break up, etc., etc.).

The mass media and the health professionals will not tell you that there is no such thing as safe sex because they designed this lie in the first place. Many of these professional are trained to uphold post-modern Darwinian theories and reject God's wise and loving instructions.

God, on the other hand, loves you too much to let you be deceived. He alone has your back. He knows the temptations you will face, but He has also given you His grace to overcome them.

Sex is a beautiful gift you shouldn't spread around. Give it to the one who really deserves it – that is, your husband or your wife! He or she will not only appreciate your decision, but will appreciate you for staying pure as well.

#8

Married But Not Special

Those who educate young people will not tell you that:

Premarital sex reduces the beauty and novelty of sex when you eventually get married.

I am so thankful to God that the first and only person I've ever been with and made love to is my wife. It was novel. It was fresh. It was beautiful. It was a journey we took together.

We've been married for over 29 years now, and I have never regretted it. We have something very special and it's still beautiful after all these years.

If it's still possible, I will encourage you to set that as a goal for your future too, because it can be extra-special. Something powerful and binding takes place when you only share your body and your deepest emotions with the one you love and no one else.

I think many of the challenges we are seeing in our society and marriages today is because we are not observing this special binding *initiation* with the person we eventually marry. So we always feel that something is missing.

I remember feeling that way when I missed my very first two Chemistry lessons in Secondary School. When I eventually attended the class, I felt like an alien, because I could not, for the life of me, grasp what was going on. And, that lost feeling haunted me until I dropped the subject altogether a couple of years later.

The first time a girl has sex with a guy, a thin membrane over her vagina (called the hymen) gets torn and a bit of blood is released. Spiritually speaking, God designed this to symbolise the sealing of a *Covenant* – with blood. It's like saying, "As we have sex for the first time, I vow to be yours forever. And, this drop of blood is to seal my vow to you". Now, that's special!

People who are sexually active before they get married have nothing that special and that precious to look forward to when they get married. How sad is that? No wonder marriages are failing at an alarming rate today. People get married, but don't feel special.

The media won't tell you this because they don't uphold the theology behind the sanctity of marriage, and many of them haven't experienced it in their own marriages, either. That's why it makes more sense to listen to someone who has, and who has no reason to short-change you.

Most of us would not feel right if we couldn't celebrate our birthdays in a special way. God gave us sex to celebrate our marriages in a special way. Don't blow your special thing on a passing friendship. It is not worth it! And, it is spectacularly foolish too!

#9

Why Buy The Cow?

Those who educate young people will not tell you that:

Men are 4 times less likely to marry a girl they are already having regular sex with. Why? Because sex before marriage greatly reduces the value guys place on girls.

More often than not, it's the girls that have more to lose when they yield to the sexual advances of guys. Even when the guys have been sexually active themselves, they still prefer to marry girls who haven't been as active as they have.

Why? Because they see sleeping around as trophies that prove their masculinity, but see girls sleeping around as shameful, dirty, and lacking in taste. So girls get the short end of the stick and have more to lose!

I can hear all the girls saying, "It's not fair!" I agree! But that's life, and life is not always fair! That's why you must learn to say 'No'. That's why you must resist the pressure and the blackmail that will come from boys who fancy you and who you fancy. You must guard your reputation and keep your legs closed until the right time.

Some years ago, a friend told me the story of a young man who was dragging his feet on the issue of marrying his girl friend. He eventually gave her an engagement ring during a cruise. Another couple on the cruise asked him when he was planning to have the wedding.

His answer was, "Not any time soon. Why pay for milk when you can have the Cow for free."

If that doesn't shock you, nothing will. But that is how many selfish young men think nowadays.

Hollywood and the mass media will not tell you that men are less likely to rush into marrying a girl they are already having regular sex with, because they are vigorously and proactively anti-marriage.

That's why in their soaps, novels, and films, they hypocritically mock stable marriages as boring and passionless; and they promote sleeping around as exciting and modern. Don't be fooled!

God wants you to get your value and your self-esteem from your relationship with Him, not from whom you are sleeping with or how many sexual partners you can entice.

As a matter of fact, God will not be pleased with you if you intentionally go out to hurt or misguide one of His special sons or daughters. Why? Because He sent His Son, Jesus Christ, to die for them. And, when you intentionally hurt that person, you are hurting their Saviour too. So be warned!

No one should take advantage of or exploit other believers... The Lord is the one who punishes people for all these things. We've already told you and warned you about this.
                    (1 Thessalonians 4:6. GWT.)

#10

Moulded By Sex

Those who educate young people will not tell you that:

Your first sexual encounters can determine the way you respond to sex for the rest of your life – negatively or positively.

Recently, I watched a TV documentary on Prostitutes and Prostitution in the United Kingdom. At one point, the host of the programme asked one of the 'working ladies' a very telling question.

She said, "Why do you allow 5 to 10 strange men to abuse you daily?"

Her answer was painful to hear. She said, "I do it because I have always felt I deserved it. I've always felt dirty and unworthy – since my uncle abused me at 10 years of age".

What she was saying is proof that the way a person is introduced to sex, can affect that person positively or negatively for a very long time.

Although she was probably around 28 years of age at the time of the interview, an event that took place 18 years before was still haunting her and informing her choices and actions.

In the same way, half-baked, booze-motivated sexual encounters between young people in the cupboard can spell trouble later on in life. Don't be that careless with your life because you want to have 3 minutes of fun.

In my estimation up to 9 out of every 10 *first* sexual intercourse encounters (outside of marriage) are awkward and problematic. Why? Well, because young people are often anxious, inexperienced, feeling guilty, and don't want to be caught in the act. In addition, if the girl is a virgin, the process of getting her virginity broken can be very painful.

The Media will not tell you that taking part in teenage sexual experiments can affect your sexual pleasure for years to come, because it is not sensational and it does not sell magazines.

God, on the other hand, is interested in the quality of your life, as well as its direction. That's why He is leading you to read this book.

You only have one life! Guard it and treasure it!!

#11

Consummate, Procreate, Lubricate

Those who educate young people will not tell you that:

The precious gift of sex was given to us for three main reasons. Anything outside of these reasons is an abuse of its original purpose.

God gave us the precious gift of sex to consummate, procreate, and lubricate. Using it for anything less is not only an abuse of its divine purpose, but a recipe for pain and unhappiness.

CONSUMMATE

The primary purpose of sex is to cement our marriage commitment. It was designed to be the one special thing we give each other to affirm and seal our marriage vows. God intended that when we make love for the first time to the one we marry, a perpetual covenant relationship would begin. Our marriage is consummated, and we become one flesh. There can be nothing more precious or beautiful than that.

PROCREATE

The second reason for the sexual act is to help bring children into a loving and affirming environment. In other words, you have to make love to have kids. Again, a lot of modern thinking and practice seeks to erode God's blueprint for healthy family life. Although having a test tube baby or getting pregnant through artificial insemination may be a helpful way to conceive a baby for some, it could be more damaging if the baby is not brought into the world by two loving and committed parents.

LUBRICATE

The final reason for sex is to oil the engine of marriage. Marriage is hard work, but it is meant to be fun too. Sex makes it fun. When the pressures of life are sky high and challenges pour in relentlessly from every corner, healthy, passionate, and caring sex can act like a reset button.

When there has been offence, conflict, or misunderstanding, good, affectionate sex reconnects you to your better self and to your loved one. The relationship is lubricated, and things can roll smoothly back into place.

Sex is to seal your lifelong commitment to your spouse. Sex is designed to make you a partner with God in the creative process of producing new life. And, sex was given to the human race to give us a taste of the joy and ecstasy of heaven on earth.

Hollywood will not tell you what God had in mind when He gave us the beautiful gift of sex, because they generally deny that He even exists. It is more in their interest if you blindly see sex as a way to fulfil your lustful desires. If you do, the benefits of consummation and lubrication may simply pass you by.

No! Sex is not for practice; it's not for sharing around; it's not for lustful exploitations; and it's certainly not for sale. Sex is for consummation, procreation, and lubrication. I can say this, because it has worked for my wife and I for the last 29 years. It has been working for the human race for the last 6000 years too.

#12

Boundaries Are Good

Those who educate young people will not tell you that:

Sexual boundaries are good for you.

If you are a young person reading this book, you need boundaries. That's why God gave you parents. Now, I know that you probably wish you didn't have to get home by 10 O Clock. You can't understand why you need to go to the Mall with a mature escort, either. But believe me, you do.

Even if you are very mature and you have good values and principles, there are always people looking to take advantage of inexperienced young boys or girls. Your parents know this; that's why they try to watch over you or set out boundaries for you.

So, you must understand that boundaries are not bad in themselves.

- They help you develop values and discipline.

- They safeguard your present and future happiness.

- They reduce your chances of making terrible mistakes.

- They protect you from a lot of emotional pain and regret.

- They keep you under your parents' covering and grace.

If you are in a relationship with the opposite sex, you need boundaries too. You need boundaries that will help to keep your relationships pure. Boundaries that will keep you from making foolish or wrong sexual choices!

If you are in a serious relationship, here are some boundaries you should discuss and agree on with your partner:

1. Avoid spending hours alone together in locked rooms.

2. Avoid sitting in cars parked in dark, isolated corners.

3. Avoid deep kissing, heavy petting, and lustful fumbling.

4. Avoid the temptation to consume alcohol when together.

5. Find ways to enjoy each other's company with other mutual friends.

6. Resist the urge to undress when you are together because things can only go one way from there.

If you are not in a serious relationship with the opposite sex, here are some boundaries you may wish to adopt too:

1. Avoid visiting friends of the opposite sex alone.

2. Don't go anywhere without telling someone responsible.

3. Don't drink anything you didn't order for yourself.

4. Avoid favours that place you in a compromising position.

5. Don't take expensive gifts from people who might want something in return.

6. If any portion of your food or drink has been left unattended at a party or a get-together, don't consume it when you return.

'Abstinence' is not a dirty word. It's a lifesaver. It gives you time to make wise decisions. When you abstain from premature and premarital sex, you save yourself from a lot of unnecessary heartaches and pain.

Hollywood doesn't mind if you sleep around. They want you to think that your parents are just cramping your style. But God wants you to know that He put parents or authority figures in your life to protect you from self-inflicted pain and regret.

Run from anything that stimulates youthful lusts. Instead, pursue righteous living, faithfulness, love, and peace. Enjoy the companionship of those who call on the Lord with pure hearts.
(2 Timothy 2:22. NLT.)

#13

A Question of Consequence

Those who educate young people will not tell you that:

Sex before marriage often attracts negative consequences because it violates God's divine order of things.

You've got to remember that no one can intentionally continue to violate God's instructions or commandments and get away with it. The Author of the Book of Romans put it more succinctly when he said, ***"The wages of sin is death..."*** (Romans 6:23.)

If you have any respect for God, you will do well to heed this truth. Pre-marital sex is never free. Someone always pays dearly for it in one way or another. So, don't let that person be you.

If things go wrong, and they very often do, you could end up with a lower quality of life. You could end up caring for children before you are ready. You could get stuck below the poverty line, with a couple of children and no spouse.

You could also develop complicated health problems with an uncertain future. Remember, you only have one life; don't ruin it. Delay gratification, and you will bypass a lot of regrets.

God's order of things is simple. You find the person you can spend the rest of your life with, get God's blessings by getting married in Church, and have all the sex you can handle for the rest of your lives. That's it. Everything else will fall in place with God's help.

Hollywood will never tell you about all the tragedies and casualties of premature, premarital sex. Nor will they make films about the painful consequences of sex before marriage. Instead, they make films to trivialise and legitimise it.

The Bible says:

> *Now the works of the flesh are evident, which are: adultery, fornication, uncleanness, lewdness, idolatry, sorcery, hatred, contentions, jealousies, outbursts of wrath, selfish ambitions, dissensions, heresies, envy, murders, drunkenness, revelries, and the like; of which I tell you beforehand, just as I also told you in time past, that those who practice such things will not inherit the kingdom of God.*
>
> (Galatians 5:19-21.)

Notice what verse 21 says emphatically: *Those who practice such things will not inherit the Kingdom of God.* Fornication or sex outside of marriage is one of such works of the flesh. It prevents you from enjoying much of what God has in stock for you. Not only in the future, but in the here and now.

God wants you to avoid the heartache and pain that come from intentionally disobeying His instructions. He also wants you to close the door on Satan's desire to 'sift you as wheat.' Don't give the devil an inch, or else he will try to rob you of a lifetime.

Your life is too precious to be vandalised by carelessness. Delay gratification and enjoy the rest of your life the way God designed it to be enjoyed. Delay gratification and be an example to your generation.

#14

The Best Kind of Sex

Sex within a responsible, loving, and committed marital relationship is the only kind that is completely good for you.

Not every kind of sexual activity is good for you. "Why?" you may ask. Because God says so many times in His Word to us! For instance, He forbids His people from having sex with animals. He forbids us from having sex with our own gender. And, He forbids us from having sex with people we are not married to.

Better still, let me show you what God says in His Word about the different types of sexual activities and exploits that people get into these days. He told Moses to give the following instructions to His people:

If you obey my decrees and my regulations, you will find life through them. I am the Lord. "You must never have sexual relations with a close relative, for I am the Lord. "Do not violate your father by having sexual relations with your mother. She is your mother; you must not have sexual relations with her. "Do not have sexual relations with any of your father's wives, for this would violate your father. "Do not have sexual relations with your sister or half sister, whether she is your father's daughter or your mother's daughter, whether she was born into your household or someone else's. "Do not have sexual relations with your granddaughter, whether she is your son's daughter or your daughter's daughter, for this would violate yourself. "Do not have sexual relations with your stepsister, the daughter of any of your father's wives, for she is your sister. "Do not have sexual relations with your father's sister, for she is your father's close relative. "Do not have sexual relations with your mother's sister, for she is your mother's close relative. "Do not violate your uncle, your father's brother, by having sexual relations with his wife, for she is your aunt. "Do not have sexual relations with your daughter-in-law; she is your son's wife, so you must not have sexual relations with her. "Do not have sexual relations with your brother's wife, for this would violate your brother. "Do not have sexual relations with both a woman and her daughter. And do not take her granddaughter, whether her son's daughter or her daughter's daughter, and have sexual relations with her. They are close relatives, and this would be a wicked act. "While your wife is living, do not marry her sister and have sexual relations with her, for they would be rivals. "Do not have sexual relations with a woman during her period of menstrual impurity. "Do not defile yourself by having sexual intercourse with your neighbour's wife. (Leviticus 18:5-20 NLT)

*"Do not practice homosexuality, having sex with
another man as with a woman. It is a detestable sin.
"A man must not defile himself by having sex with an
animal. And a woman must not offer herself to a
male animal to have intercourse with it. This is a
perverse act. "Do not defile yourselves in any of these
ways, for the people I am driving out before you have
defiled themselves in all these ways. Whoever
commits any of these detestable sins will be cut off
from the community of Israel. So obey my
instructions, and do not defile yourselves by
committing any of these detestable practices that
were committed by the people who lived in the land
before you. I am the Lord your God."* (Leviticus 18:22-
24, 29, 30. NLT)

*"Don't you realize that those who do wrong will not
inherit the Kingdom of God? Don't fool yourselves.
Those who indulge in sexual sin... or commit
adultery, or are male prostitutes, or practice
homosexuality... —none of these will inherit the
Kingdom of God."* (1 Corinthians 6:9-10. NLT)

*"Run from sexual sin! No other sin so clearly affects
the body as this one does. For sexual immorality is a
sin against your own body. 19 Don't you realize that
your body is the temple of the Holy Spirit, who lives
in you and was given to you by God? You do not
belong to yourself, for God bought you with a high
price. So you must honor God with your body.* (1
Corinthians 6:18-20. NLT)

"God's will is for you to be holy, so stay away from all sexual sin." (1 Thessalonians 4:3 NLT)

Nothing can be clearer! God says that these sexual practices are detestable. They are repugnant. They are offensive and they are an abomination to Him. Hollywood will not tell you this because they need to be politically correct, but I am telling you, because I know that God is never wrong and something negative always results from intentionally disobeying Him.

#15

Depraved Emotions

Watching sexually explicit materials does to your emotions what drugs do to your brain.

When you turn on the news and read of sexually depraved people who sexually assault their victims; or who snatch children off the street, rape them, and then kill them; or who take pleasure in looking at horrific pictures of babies being abused online – I am sure you feel sick. And you should!

But it may be more helpful to ask yourself how they got there in the first place. They certainly weren't born that way. Well, I'll tell you how. Almost 100% of the time, these depraved kidnappers, rapists, and paedophiles start out on pornography and explicit sexual materials.

After reading some News clips of recent offenders, I noticed that each rapist, kidnapper, or murderer who was caught for doing any of these despicable things, also had plenty of explicit images on their laptops or computers. They were all frequent visitors to porn or child abuse sites, and they all had earlier reports or convictions for sexually motivated crimes.

My point is simple: Watching sexually explicit material is addictive. Pornography is addictive. And, although not everyone who engages in it will turn into a rapist or paedophile, most will get addicted to some degree. Some will use it to masturbate and may end up craving unrealistic sexual fantasies.

Either way, the consequence of pornography in your head, or in your sexual choices, promises to cause pain.

Pornography messes up your emotions. It gives you false highs and painful lows. Consuming sexually explicit materials is like a drug. It promises so much, but delivers so little. It turns you on for a little while, and then leaves you dry and wanting more.

Pornography is a destructive habit because it destroys marriages. It is addictive because it leaves you craving for more. It is shameful because people (who could easily be your siblings or family members) have been exploited to produce those explicit materials.

Pornography is expensive. It is draining. But, worst of all, it alienates you from God.

People who consume pornography can't pray. They can't hold their head up because the critic inside them is constantly accusing them. They are afraid to be around spiritually mature people.

They miss wholesome places (like their Church) because they feel guilty. They live a double life, and they have to hide their shameful antics from everyone around them.

The 'powers that be' will not tell you these things, because they are often addicted to it themselves. They will not teach young people these things because they benefit in some way from the sexual exploitation industry.

But God wants you to know it, so that you can avoid unnecessary heartache and misery.

He wants you to understand what you are doing and what it is doing to you – so that you can ask for His forgiveness and His grace to break the habit, if you habitually indulge in it.

"God has called us to live holy lives, not impure lives. Therefore, anyone who refuses to live by these rules is not disobeying human teaching but is rejecting God, who gives his Holy Spirit to you."

(1 Thessalonians 4:7-8. NLT)

#16

Attracting the Right Person

Inner beauty and respect is what attracts the right kind of man. Love and kindness is what attracts the right kind of lady.

Young people are often of the false opinion that they can attract the right guy or girl into their lives by what they wear; or what they drive; or how expensive their shoes are; or how classy or provocative they dress.

- That's why the latest fashion is so important to most young people.

- That's why people get into debt trying to live way beyond their means.

- That's why young people love to show off their flashy cars to the opposite sex.

- That's why young people flirt with one another at parties or social gatherings.

- That's why many young people wear the most revealing and suggestive clothing they can find when they are going out.

Unfortunately, this behaviour merely causes young people to see each other as cheap objects to lust after and use. If you turn yourself into a sex object for the opposite sex, they will simply treat you as one.

I want you to understand that no serious-minded guy ever plans to marry a girl he sees as loose and shameless. Similarly, no serious girl wants to get attached to a guy she sees as arrogant, vain and full-of-himself.

In 1 Peter 3:3-5, the writer teaches us what works:

Don't be so concerned about the outward beauty that depends on fancy hairstyles, expensive jewellery, or beautiful clothes. Instead, be known for the beauty that comes from within, the unfading beauty of a gentle and quiet spirit, which is so precious to God. That is the way the holy women of old made themselves beautiful...

Inner beauty is what attracts a good man to you. Not a nice dress, or expensive shoes, or borrowed jewellery, or exposing yourself and leaving nothing to the imagination.

In the same way, ladies are mostly attracted to guys that are kind and caring. Showing off your hairy chest or your new ride only appeals to shallow girls. They cannot ultimately make you happy when the going gets tough.

Hollywood will not tell you this, because they've chosen to peddle a philosophy of shallowness based on lust and ignorance. The media and the pharmaceutical companies will not tell you this either, because they too back and promote the sexual exploitation of young people.

God, on the other hand, wants you to know the truth, because it is the truth you know that sets you free. Truth frees you to be yourself. It frees you to be authentic, credible, confident, alive, joyful, and even peaceful. Truth empowers you to stay true to yourself, instead of trying to be like your friends.

God wants you to know that inward beauty trumps outward appearance. He also wants you to know that character trumps fancy toys – every time.

If you want to find a godly partner to spend the rest of your life with, do it God's way, not society's way. With the help of the Holy Spirit, work on being beautiful and charming within. Work on being an authentic person. Work on your character. Work on the way you talk to people. Work on being positive. Work on being kind, loving, and caring.

If you do things, and do them God's way, you will enjoy divine help all through life. Things will just work out for you and you will be an example to your generations. Isn't that what you really want?

And we know that God causes everything to work together for the good of those who love God and are called according to his purpose for them.

(Romans 8:28. NLT)

#17

Potential for Divorce

As sex outside of marriage has increased in our society, so also has the rate of divorce and dissatisfaction in marriage.

Many of society's ills can be traced back to the breakdown in the family unit. From the skyrocketing prison population to the increase in urban gang culture, the disintegration of the family is the pivotal reason.

There is one important statistic that gets shoved under the table a lot. And that is the link between the explosion in sex outside of marriage and the increase in the rate of divorce a few years latter.

The statistics show that the sexual revolution that took place between the 1960s and the 1980s corresponds roughly to the increase in divorce between the 1970s and the 1990s.

Why? Because recreational sex sets young people up to be unfaithful later on in life!

After all, if it was okay to have five or six sexual partners before marriage, what's to stop you from having one or two more sexual partners when your spouse is unavailable or upset with you? What's to stop you from jumping into bed with one of your old boyfriends or girlfriends?

That's precisely what happens 80% of the time. A couple hit a low patch in their relationship (due to stress, work, children, money, or conflict), and either partner simply goes out to get his/her sexual needs met somewhere else.

It's called being unfaithful, having an affair, cheating on your spouse, and a dozen other negative connotations. But in spite of our liberated sexual worldview, nobody likes to see his or her partner run off to sleep with someone else. Well, that's why marriages are collapsing at an alarming rate in our society.

My point is simple: Sleeping around desensitises you to the virtues of monogamy. It can turn you into an amoral creature with no sense of commitment or shame. And, worst of all, it connects you to others who have similar scruples.

Sex outside of marriage is living on the edge. It demeans you, defiles you, demotes you, and disappoints you. Sex outside of marriage is a cheap imitation. It opens a door of dissatisfaction in your soul.

Neither Hollywood nor the Media will tell you this, but the statistics don't lie. More and more people are struggling to stay faithful (or stay married) on the aftermath of the world's greatest sexual revolution. Once the true reason for this state of affairs become clear, people will understand why God frowns at fornication, adultery, homosexually, lust and many other sexual vices: They simply desensitise us to the godly ideals of faithfulness, commitment and perseverance.

#18

A Small Fraction of Love

Sex is so overrated, because it only accounts for a fraction of the act of love and lovemaking.

If you think that sex is lovemaking, you are dead wrong. Sex is sex, but lovemaking is something entirely different. Lovemaking may eventually progress to sex, but sex is just the 'icing on the cake'. Lovemaking is the cake!

Sex is a fraction of lovemaking – and a small fraction, indeed. What makes lovemaking really fantastic and enjoyable are the things you say to each other and the ways you treat each other long before you have sex.

Great lovemaking is built on the foundation of kind words, caring gestures, loving romance, patience, and understanding – just to mention a few. That's why, if you are feeling insecure in a relationship, sex will not fulfil you. If you are feeling used and abused, sex will only make you more miserable.

Sex is an event, but lovemaking is a process. Sex can be done and over with in 3 minutes, but lovemaking takes time. It really takes a lifetime!

Lovemaking grows and gets more fulfilling as it matures. Lovemaking actually increases your love and appreciation for your spouse. That's why sex outside of marriage cannot serve you like sex in a loving marriage can.

Sex is overrated, but true lovemaking is only experienced by a few. You can be in that number if you take to heart what I am teaching you in this book. You can enjoy your sex life – as God intended – by waiting for the right time and the right person.

Good sex is multidimensional. The conditions need to be right; your partner needs to be right; and the techniques employed need to suit the two of you. The technical aspects of sex are beyond the scope of this book, but when the time comes, understanding what you are doing may help increase your sexual pleasure. When that time comes, there are many helpful books and materials out there. Find one that suits you and your spouse.

Why the blockbuster films our young people watch never seemed to carry this kind of balanced true-life message is anyone's guess. My guess is that many filmmakers are more interested in sensationalism than in the education of young people.

God, on the other hand, loves you too much to leave you in the pit of ignorance. That's why He chose me to get this simple message out to you. That message is:

Sex is so overrated. Therefore, don't be a sex object, be a lovemaker! The gap between the two of them is like night and day.

#19

Depressed And Suicidal

Those who educate young people will not tell you that:

Being Sexually Active can lead to Depression and Suicidal tendencies

Being sexually active (especially amongst young girls) is known to increase their rate of depression and tendency to be suicidal. Dr. Meg Meeker, who treats all kinds of sexually active girls in her clinic, recently said, "One of the major causes of depression in my patients is sex…"

She further went on to explain that "Teenage sexual activity routinely leads to emotional turmoil and psychological distress".

In a recent study of over 20,000 adolescents by The National Longitudinal Survey of Adolescent Health, just over a quarter (25.3%) of sexually active girls were identified as depressed; compared to 7.7% amongst those who were not sexually active.

In a similar study, 14.3% of girls who were sexually active attempted suicide in one year. The average for teens that were not sexually active was 5%. In other words, active premarital sex increases the risk of depression and suicide three-fold.

Why is something that is supposed to be so desirable and enjoyable causing so much pain and depression amongst sexually active teens? The reasons are numerous, but let me just leave you with five:

1.) **Sexually active teens know that what they are doing is not right.** That's why they hide it from their parents and from people who love them and are looking out for them. Their sense of guilt merely increases their stress levels and their anxiety.

2.) **Sexually active teens know that they are really being used and sometimes abused.** This is especially true for many girls. They give in to sex hoping to gain the heart and commitment of the guys they are with, but 9 out of 10 times, the relationship falls apart faster than you can say Coca-Cola. The guys leave and those feelings of being abandoned and abused settle in for good.

3.) **Sexually active teens know that they are compromising their own inner guiding system.** We call that inner guiding system, the conscience. If you talk to sexually active young people, they will often tell you that they didn't feel ready for sex, but they were under a lot of pressure to yield. That can't be good for anyone caught in such a confusing vicious cycle.

4.) **Sexually active teens are often on pregnancy prevention medications that produce depressive symptoms and side effects.** Any medication or drug that is designed to depress or tamper with a ladies reproductive system, will invariably mess with her emotions also.

5.) **Sexually active teens who have been introduced to the scriptures have the additional guilt of knowing**

that they are displeasing God. When we intentionally do the things that displease God, we carry guilt like a sack of large rocks around our necks. And, those rocks stay put, until we repent of the sin and change our ways.

That's why the Bible tells us to:

Flee sexual immorality! "Every sin that a man does is outside the body," but he who commits sexual immorality sins against his own body.

(1 Corinthians 6:18.)

You see, sex complicates things when you are young. It wasn't designed for young people who just want to have fun. God gave us sex to consummate our commitment to each other, to procreate & produce children, and to lubricate and enjoy our union continuously.

Unfortunately, many young people today view sex as a fun activity they can share with anyone they fancy. And, because they don't understand the purpose of sex, they abuse it.

When you abuse the one gift God gave you to share with one special committed person, you hurt yourself now and you deprive that person from really being special in the future.

The so-called sexual revolution in our society today, is not really a revolution, but a humiliation. Reason? It's destroying our young people's self-esteem, identity, sexuality, expectations, health, careers and morality. Premarital sex also has the potential to negatively impact on our future marriage and family life – since the way we are introduced to sex leaves an indelible mark on our souls.

It's easy to see how all this pressure and complication can lead to stress, anxiety, depression, alcohol and drug abuse, and suicidal tendencies in young people. But things don't have to be that way with you. That's why I am letting you know what the deal is up-front.

I may not know who you are, but I know that if you imbibe the world's permissive views of sex, you will hurt yourself and anyone you have sex with. That is simply the consequence of disobeying God and doing things your own way.

The Media will not tell you that being sexually active (when you are too young to fully appreciate the complications and consequences) can lead to depression and suicidal tendencies; but I am sharing this truth with you because I care about you and don't want to see you caught in a worldly trap that is totally avoidable.

#20

Empowered to Wait

You can abstain from having premature sex until you get married, because God gives special grace to those who desire to honour Him in this way.

Too many young people fail to stay sexually pure because they try to abstain by their own power or their own will. Self-control is a great thing to have, but there are some situations that call for more than self-control. Trying to stay sexually pure is one of those situations!

That's why the Bible instructs us to flee from sexual sins.

Flee sexual immorality. Every sin that a man does is outside the body, but he who commits sexual immorality sins against his own body. Or do you not know that your body is the temple of the Holy Spirit who is in you, whom you have from God, and you are not your own? For you were bought at a price; therefore glorify God in your body and in your spirit, which are God's. (1 Corinthians 6:18-20.)

Notice, we are not instructed to resist or apply self-control when it comes to sexual sins. We are commanded to flee. Flee means to run or escape for dear life.

"Why is this so important?" you may ask. It's important because your ability to 'resist or exercise self-control' is often weaker than the 'temptation' to indulge your feelings.

That's why you need God's help too. He wants to give you the ability to stay sexually pure, if you sincerely ask Him to. Your job, of course, is to make sure you are not putting yourself in sexually compromising situations.

Even if you've been sexually active in the past, but want to honour God and stay sexually pure from now until you get married, God's grace will make it possible. Just ask Him to help you in prayer! Believe He has heard and answered you!! Then live a sexually pure life!!!

Young people, I'm challenging you to answer the call to keep yourself sexually pure until you get married. That is God's blueprint for sexual fulfilment and happiness. It's also His blueprint for a regret-free life.

Hollywood will not tell you that you can 'abstain' from premature sex until you get married. Indeed, they would rather have you doing the opposite. But God is clear on what works best. And, that is 'abstinence.' Not because He doesn't want you to enjoy your life, but because He wants to protect you from all the dreadful consequences of allowing your flesh to control your behaviour.

Do not let sin control the way you live; do not give in to its lustful desires. Do not let any part of your body become a tool of wickedness, to be used for sinning. Instead, give yourselves completely to God since you have been given new life. And use your whole body as a tool to do what is right for the glory of God. (Romans 6:12-13.)

Sex is good and sex is great, but sex is best for those who wait – Rev. Tony Peters

#21

Turn A New Leaf

God can heal you of any sexual failures and empower you to start out afresh.

The fact that you may have failed sexually in the past doesn't mean that you have to continue to fail into the future. We all start out as helpless sinners, and we've all done things we are not proud of.

But when you come over to God's side (through faith in the death and resurrection of Jesus Christ), old things do pass away. Also, all things have the potential to become new, if that is what you really want for your life.

What a blessing to know that the past no longer has to interfere with your future. That's why the Bible puts it this way: ***"If anyone belongs to Christ, he or she is a new person. The old life is gone; a new life has begun."***

(2 Corinthians 5:17.) NLT

That simply means you can start out afresh. It means you can turn a new leaf. It means you can experience the total forgiveness and healing that comes from God.

The media and the pharmaceutical companies will not tell you that God is a Healer and a Restorer. The Hollywood will not tell you that God erases past mistakes when you sincerely repent of them before Him.

I want you to know that God will not only forgive and heal any past sexual failures, but He would empower you to start out afresh. He would give you a clean slate to 'live' on. That means you can now abstain from premature, premarital, and pre-blessed sex. You can now choose to do things God's way.

If you've been fortunate and have not made any sexual blunders yet, God is able and willing to keep you pure to the very end. Just trust Him to help you say 'No.'

God is able to keep you from stumbling and falling.

"Now all glory to God, who is able to keep you from falling away and will bring you with great joy into his glorious presence without a single fault. All glory to him who alone is God, our Saviour through Jesus Christ our Lord. All glory, majesty, power, and authority are his before all time, and in the present, and beyond all time! Amen."

(Jude 1:24-25.)

CONCLUSION

4 Reasons the Movers-and-Shakers of our Society will not tell you what I have been trying to show you in this book

1.) **It would reduce their profits – big time!**

Sex is big business. And, if the multibillion-dollar industries that benefit from the mass sexual experiment, advertised what they know about its dangers, their profits would plummet drastically.

Sex sells! It fills theatres too. That's why almost every box-office film is engineered to include sexually explicit scenes or content.

The Pharmaceutical industry is a £100 billion industry; and a sizable part of their income comes from drugs manufactured to combat the consequences of a liberal sexualised culture encouraged by Hollywood.

They have no moral incentive to tell you what they know about your sexual choices because (to some extent) your ignorance is the reason for a good fraction of their business. The profits from drugs created for abortions, pregnancy and pregnancy prevention, and treatments for sexually transmitted diseases (to mention a few) are huge.

Then there is the Porn industry. No one knows exactly how much they rake in every year, but it is definitely not chicken-change. What's my point? Simply, that sex is big business! Those in the know, don't care who gets hurt or squashed or damaged in the process – as long as money keeps flowing their way.

2.) It would negate their attempt to cheapen sex and glamorise immorality.

Giant multi-national companies & the popular Media will not tell you what I have shared with you in this book, because it would negate their clear agenda to glamorising and cheapening sex.

One of the most destructive lies we have been told – again and again – in the last 50 years by the so-called experts, is that sex is merely a physical activity between two consenting people (...even when the consenting people are children).

The truth, however, is that sex is far more complex and intricate. Sex is spiritual; it is emotional; it is physiological and it is psychological. It usually has financial implications too.

Sex is a process (not just an event), designed by our Creator to make two committed people inseparable and completely loyal too each other for life. Another way of saying this is that sex was designed to connect two people together inextricably.

So don't be fooled! These institutions know that if we buy into the theory that sex is no more binding than a handshake, we would hop from bed to bed and keep their industry booming.

3.) They don't really care very much about young people's health or future anyway.

The giant multinational companies & the popular Media will not tell you what I have been sharing with you in this book because they care more about their profits and their bottom-line than about really helping people like you.

Making drugs to help you combat STD is not the same as teaching or helping you to avoid the disease altogether.

Another way to look at this issue is to ask the question, "Could the gate-keepers of our health institutions and our Governments be doing a better job at helping young people to reduce the pain and regret of a sexually active culture?"

The answer to me is a definite 'yes'. But it hasn't happened yet because some well-placed 'heavy weights' will lose out financially; and that preposition is not acceptable to them.

4.) A healthy part of their profit comes from the mistakes of young people.

The giant multinational companies & the popular Media will not tell you what I am teaching you in this book, because your mistakes in many ways are their gain.

For instance, when young people are sad or confused or disappointed, they drink more, smoke more or experiment more with drugs. They get into more debt. They get more careless. They medicate more. And, they have more accidents.

Who benefits when young people do these foolish things? The pharmaceutical companies, the drug barons, the breweries, the media, the moneylenders, and the tobacco moguls – come to mind.

- If you get pregnant before you are ready to nurse a child, they profit.

- If you fail your exams, drop out of school and become depressed, they profit.

- If you lose your job and have to depend on government hand-outs, they profit.

- If you get sick or infected with a virus or sexually transmitted disease, they profit.

- If you get heartbroken or feel used by someone who doesn't love you, they profit.

- If you can't have a child naturally in the future and have to opt for IVF treatment, they profit.

- If you become ill or depressed because your life was unexpectedly put on hold, they profit, regardless!

You Only Get One Chance At Life

Here is how I see things: Life is fragile, and you only get one chance to live it out. You only have to make one silly mistake and the whole of your life can tumble to the bottom of the ocean of life, like the Titanic.

On the other hand, you only have to make a few prudent choices and you can be lifted to the highest heavens. Make a few godly commitments and you can have the things you've always wanted in life. Surely then, it makes good sense to make those choices wisely.

I made one major decision when I was 16 years old, and I am still enjoying the fruit of that decision 38 years on.

"What decision was that?" I hear you ask.

Well, it was the decision to **embrace** and **follow** God's direction for my life – by sincerely asking **Jesus Christ** to be my Lord and to take His **rightful** place in my **heart**. I can tell you that this was life changing for me at the time, but was worth it.

Over the next few years, my **mind-set** changed. My heart's **desires** changed. My **attitude** changed. And, my **destiny** changed too.

What God did for me all those years ago, He can do it for you too– because He is not partial. He simply looks into your heart and rewards you with what He know is best for you– if you would choose to do things His way.

That's why I am encouraging you to make this **decision** too. I encourage you to turn everything over to Him, **humble** yourself, **repent** of your sins, **ask** for His forgiveness, and **receive** His gift of Eternal Life.

I'm not talking about an emotional or religious response that's only skin-deep. I am asking you to **trust** God for a heart transformation, so that you desire to do things God's way.

That, in my humble opinion is what every young person needs. That is the doorway into all that you'll ever want or need in life. Don't just take my word for it; try it out for yourself.

Hollywood will not tell you that Jesus **paid** the ultimate price for you to have a good life. The Media will not tell you that **faith** in God plays a major role in the choices you make. The government may not warn you to take your spiritual life seriously if you want to survive in this decadent jungle called earth. But, I am!

I am asking you to make sure you are **right** with God. Make sure you are not just playing religious games. Make sure you are thoroughly **'Born Again'**. Because the One who created all things said, *"You must be born again"*. (John 3:7.)

If you don't know what all this means or how to acquire it, find a life-giving Church and ask the minister there to walk you through the **steps to salvation**.

So what would it be for you? The Hollywood code or the Bible code? The Media's lies or God's eternal truth? The choice is yours, but I wrote this book to help you make the right choice. If you choose to do life God's way, my work here is done.

> *"Today I have given you the choice between life and death, between blessings and curses. Now I call on heaven and earth to witness the choice you make. Oh, that you would choose life, so that you and your descendants might live.*
>
> (Deuteronomy 30:19.)

> *"The LORD bless you and keep you; the LORD make His face shine upon you, and be gracious to you; the LORD lift up His countenance upon you, and give you peace."*
>
> (Number 6:24-26.)

Prayer of Salvation:

Say this prayer from your heart to receive Jesus Christ into your life today:

Almighty God, thank You for loving me and sending Your Son to die for me on a Cross. I wholeheartedly repent of everything I have done to offend You, and I ask You to please forgive me for rebelling against Your Word in the past.

I believe that You have a better plan for my life, so I submit myself to Your plan and Your will for my life from today.

Thank You for promising to hear my prayer, for forgiving me, and for making me Your son/daughter.

I believe that I now belong to You and that You now live in my heart. I ask it all in the precious name of Jesus Christ. Amen!

PS: If you said the prayer above from you heart, you have entered into a relationship with God, through His Son, Jesus Christ. Find a good Bible-believing Church where you can grow as a true Christian. Finally, share your decision with a mature Christian who can help you understand the Christian faith better. It's never too late to start out afresh.

****

If it's not too much to ask, please drop me an email at **tony@thekingshouse.co.uk** to let me know how this book has helped you. I'd be glad to read your testimonial.

Notes

Notes

Notes

Notes

**Other Books by the Rev. Tony Peters
on Amazon and all good Book Outlets:**

Secrets of a Lasting Marriage – 7 Vital Building Blocks for a Healthy Marriage

How to Build a Rock Solid Marriage – Choices That Will Give You the Marriage of Your Dreams

Ten Keys to Effective Communication in Marriage

Maximising Your Season of Singleness – Using Your Season of Singleness to Prepare for Marriage

Keeping God At The Centre Of Your Marriage – Simple Ways To Keep God At The Centre Of Your Relationship

How to Rescue Your Marriage from Breaking Up – Avoiding the Ten Major Relationship Killers

Stress No More – 20 Healthy Ways To Reduce Stress, Anxiety & Worry In Your Life

Find Your Life Partner God's Way – And Say Goodbye To The Dating Game

Understand Your Marriage Vows - What the Marriage Vows Mean and How to Honour Them

Why God Wants You & Your Family in a Life-giving Church – 12 Reasons to Get Involved in a Great Local Church in Your Area

Why Can't We Talk About It? - 4 Practical Steps to Help Reduce Misunderstandings During Conversations by Shola Peters

How to Find a Life-giving Church – You Can Thrive in

Why God wants you & your Family in a Life-giving Church.

From the Author
Thank you again for purchasing this book.
If you enjoyed reading it (and I certainly hope you did),
I would appreciate it if you would rate it fairly for me
and for the benefit of other potential readers. Please
post a short review on any of the sites that sell it.

Thank you very much!

All my books are available at **www.amazon.co.uk**
and all good **books outlets**.

www.rocksolidmarriages.com